Grow Page *by Carolyn Grey*

MATERIALS: Cardstock (Iris, Light Purple, Dark Green) • Purple floral vellum • *JewelCraft* (6 Silver 6mm nailheads; Lavender seed beads; FabricPuff appliques - 6 Purple flower, Dark Green border) • *Cock-A-Doodle* cursive font • *Scrap Pagerz* party lettering template • Chalk pencils (Green, Purple, Pink)

TIPS: Make Black and White copy of color photo on White cardstock and color with pencils. Cut leaves from border and place behind flowers. Glue beads for flower centers. Use a flower for the O in 'GROW'. Attach nailheads to corners.

Add-Ons

Add-Ons give memory pages exciting dimension in just seconds. Simply apply FabricPuff or Caviar Bead appliques, ribbon or embossed paper cutouts!

All American Kid *by Carolyn Grey*

MATERIALS: Cardstock (Red, White, Blue) • *Renae Lindgren* baby plaid paper • *JewelCraft* (3 sizes of Red, White & Blue FabricPuff star appliques ; 3 small, 5 medium, 1 large Silver star nailheads; Red, White, Blue beads) • 26 gauge Silver wire • *Cock-A-Doodle* cursive font • Blue chalk • Pop dot

TIPS: Tear edges of White cardstock and shade with chalk. String beads on wire. Place large star on pop dot and hook wire over top.

Garden Page *by Valoree Albert*

MATERIALS: Cardstock (White, Hunter Green) • *JewelCraft* FabricPuff appliques (bright flowers, bright butterflies) • Wire (24 gauge Green, 28 gauge Tinned Copper) • Stickers (ladybugs, dragonflies, seeds) • Wire cutters • Round-nose pliers • Craft knife • 1/16" hole punch • Wire Worker tool with small dowel • Black fine tip pen

TIPS: Place White cardstock at top. Mount photos on White and Hunter Green. Write caption on White, mount on Hunter Green.

For journal, cut 5 pieces of White. Leave 1/4" on left edge of each page for binding. Cut tabs on tops of first 4 pages and apply checkerboard and word stickers to each page. Place flower appliques on front page. Trace shape of right flower. Cut out with craft knife through 4 pages. Glue one flower applique to last page. Glue other flowers to front. Tear strips of Hunter Green cardstock for stems. Accent journal pages with stickers.

For book binding, stack pages and punch holes on left side. Use wire worker tool to make Green coil. Make as many rotations as holes. Before removing coil from dowel, stretch to length of journal. Thread coil through top hole and twist until all holes are threaded. Trim any excess wire and coil ends with pliers.

Mount journal on Hunter Green and on page. Accent page with stickers and butterfly appliques. Accent butterflies with hand looped wire. Coil ends with pliers.

Joy Title *by Delores Frantz*

MATERIALS: Red cardstock • *JewelCraft* (Round rhinestones - 4 Ruby 4mm, 5 Emerald 8mm, Ruby 8mm) • 6" of ⅛" Red ribbon • *Sizzix* die cutter and alphabet dies • Mini glue dots

Joy Page *by Deb Ringquist*

MATERIALS: *DMD* cardstock (embossed Christmas design, Dark Green, White, Dark Red) • *JewelCraft* (True Love beads; Silver 4mm flat nailheads; 4mm round rhinestones - 2 Topaz, 2 Peridot, Emerald, 4 Amethyst, 2 Rose, 2 Light Amethyst, 2 Crystal, Jonquil, 4 Sapphire; Ruby rhinestones - six 4mm, five 8mm, five 10mm) • 24 gauge Green wire • Wire Worker tool • *Fiskars* 12" paper trimmer • Mouse pad • Thumbtack • *Forster* craft stick • Black marker • Mini glue dots • *Gem-Tac* Adhesive • *Hermafix* squares

TIPS: Crop and mat photo using White and Red cardstock. Cut 2 holly borders, stars, mittens, 'Joy' and Christmas tree from embossed cardstock. Attach Red rhinestones to holly with glue dots. Place 'Joy' title on mouse pad. Using thumb, insert nailhead into paper. Turn over and use craft stick to bend prongs flat. Attach title and border to page with Hermafix. Attach star applique to star in title. Make holes in Joy and through top of each mitten. Insert 6" of wire through title box and mittens. Using smallest mandrel of the wire worker, make coils in ends. Attach mittens to page with Hermafix. Attach star appliques to mittens and one star. Attach Red rhinestone to star on tree. Attach assorted beads and rhinestones to tree with Gem-Tac. Attach tree to cardstock with Hermafix.

Princess Page *by Deb Ringquist*

MATERIALS: *DMD* cardstock (Pink, White) • *Paper Adventures* Parfait Pink al fresco paper • *SRM* 'Li'l Princess' border stickers • *JewelCraft* (Diamond mirrors - four 7mm x 3mm, eleven 16mm x 6mm, five 25mm x 11mm; Rhinestones - 7 Crystal 4mm, 24 Rose 4mm, 2 Crystal 8mm, 2 Rose hearts, 2 Rose navettes) • *Fiskars* 12" paper trimmer • *Coluzzle* square template • Craft knife • *Hermafix* • Mini glue dots • Black fine tip pen

TIPS: Crop and mat pictures. Cut Pink cardstock slightly larger than border and attach to top. Cut 1" strip of Pink cardstock, place in center of 2 border stickers and attach to bottom. Attach photos to paper. Cut 1" x 3" piece of White cardstock for journal. Cut Pink cardstock slightly larger than White and attach to page. Add mirrors and rhinestones as shown.

Illuminate Flower Pattern

Happy Holidays *by Erin Terrell*

MATERIALS: Cardstock (Green, Dark Green, Brown, Red) • Paper (*Provo Craft* Buttercream watercolor, *ColorWheel* Apple screen and Apple dot, *Keeping Memories Alive* Dark Green weave, screen, plaid and dot) • *Provo Craft* ¾" Red letter stickers • *Offray* ribbon (¼" Green, ⅛" Red) • Assorted *JewelCraft* rhinestones • *Scrap Pagerz* Christmas tree template • Brown chalk • Double-sided tape • Mini glue dots

TIPS: Make background using Green and Dark Green cardstock. Mat photo on Red. Make tree using template and Dark Green screen paper. Attach rhinestones to tree with glue dots. Cut Red and Green paper packages. Tape ribbon on packages, tie bow and attach with glue dots. Make title with letter stickers.

Birthday Girl *by Valoree Albert*

MATERIALS: Cardstock (Blue, White, Yellow) • *Making Memories* plaid papers (Magenta, Lime, Blue) • Iridescent paper • *JewelCraft* (Four 25mm x 11mm diamond mirrors; Blue Metallic Iris sequins-by-the-yard; Eyelets - 3 small and 1 large Silver, 1 large Red, 2 small Baby Blue) • Eyelet setter • Lettering templates (*EK Success* kindergarten, *Provo Craft* block) • *EK Success* pompom punch • Silver cord • Craft knife

TIPS: Mount photo on Blue cardstock, attach to page. Cut title letters from Blue and Magenta plaid. Overlap top right corner of photo with letter G. Cut strips of Blue and Magenta for candles. Mount mirrors on Yellow and trim leaving narrow border. Assemble candles. Cut White cardstock, vellum and Iridescent paper for gift bag. Set 2 Blue eyelets at top of bag and thread cord for handle. Attach sequins to bottom. Punch 3 Blue pompoms and mount on corners of photo with small Silver eyelets. Set Silver eyelet over 'i' in birthday and Red eyelet in center of R in GIRL.

Birthday Girl Candle Patterns

Birthday Girl Bag Diagram

3"

5/8" 1/2"

4 1/2"

Trim Placement

1/2"

Rhinestones & Jewels

Mirror shapes, rhinestones and jewels sparkle and shimmer on pages filled with the joy of special moments.

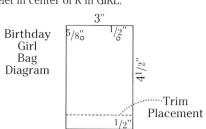

Illuminate Page *by Erin Terrell*

MATERIALS: 2 sheets of Black cardstock • *Bravissimo* Purple vellum • Amethyst Radiant Pearls • Black embossing powder • *JewelCraft* (10 Emerald triangle rhinestones; 10mm rhinestones - 15 Ruby, 10 Rose; Bugle beads - Pink/Purple, Green multi) • 26 gauge Bare Copper wire • Vargas font • Sponge • Lavender gel pen • *Crafter's Pick* Memory Mount glue • Embossing pen

TIPS: Tear 2 strips of Black for bottom of page. Sponge Radiant Pearls over strips and photo mat, let dry. String beads on wire and shape into flower stems and border. Attach rhinestones for flowers and leaves. Print title on vellum, pour embossing powder on ink and heat to set.

The Prettiest of All
by Valoree Albert

MATERIALS: Cardstock (White, Gold, Purple) • *Mary Engelbreit©* (Purple print paper, ½" White letter stickers, coordinating border stickers) • *JewelCraft* 40mm x 30mm oval mirror; 14 assorted rhinestones; Violet Metallic Iris sequins-by-the-yard • Curiz MT font • Glue dots

TIPS: Trim print paper for title. Accent top and bottom with border stickers. Apply rhinestone accents. Cut out letters to spell 'prettiest'. Adhere to center of border. Use small letter stickers to form the words 'the, of, all' for title. Mount photos on White mats and Purple strip. Outline strip with sequins using glue dots. Print journaling and mount on Gold and background paper. Accent with rhinestones. Cut girl and frog from background paper. Cut scepter from hand to allow space for mirror. Glue under other hand. Attach small rhinestone to tip of scepter. Cut mirror back from Purple and attach oval mirror, place in girl's hand. Glue Crystal rhinestones to glasses.

The Prettiest Mirror Pattern

Green Jewel Border
by Delores Frantz

MATERIALS: Cardstock (Moss Green, Yellow) • *JewelCraft* (5 Jonquil 12.7mm square rhinestones; 16 Green Metallic Iris 5mm sequins; 16 Pale Green seed beads) • Beading needle and thread • Stamp scissors • Mini glue dots

TIP: Secure sequins and beads by sewing through cardstock with needle and thread.

Daa-ling Page *by Valoree Albert*

MATERIALS: Cardstock (Black, White) • Iridescent Green and Silver paper • *Paper Adventures* ¾" Silver letter stickers • *JewelCraft* (5 assorted rhinestones; Two 9mm round mirrors) • Black fine tip pen

TIPS: Mount photos on White cardstock and trim leaving a thin border. Mount Iridescent paper and page. Print journaling on White and mount on Iridescent paper. Accent journaling with rhinestones. Create title with letter stickers. Make o's in Look with mirrors.

Card with Tag

by Beverley Morgan

MATERIALS: *DMD* (5" x 7" card, medium tag, 4½" x 6" piece of Aqua cardstock) • *Stamp Craft* bugs rubber stamp • *Color Box* Purple pigment ink pad • *Radiant Pearls* (Twilight Time, Peacock, Wild Orchid, Miners Nugget) • Clear embossing powder • *JewelCraft* (Nailheads - 4 Gold 8mm filigree, 2 Gold 6mm filigree; Navette rhinestones - 8 Sapphire, 6 Topaz; Peace sign charm) • Gold ribbon • 26 gauge Gold wire • Stipple brushes • Heat gun • Mini glue dots • Wire cutters • Round-nose pliers • Mouse pad • Craft stick

TIPS: Apply Radiant Pearls to tag and emboss following manufacturer's instructions. Place Aqua cardstock at an angle. Open card, place on mouse pad and push nailhead into corners of cardstock to secure. Turn card over and press nailhead ends flat with craft stick. Place ribbon across card, measure and mark angles, cut and adhere with glue dots. Randomly stamp dragonfly on ribbon and card. Cut 12" of wire, slip wire through hole in tag, center ends and twist together. Attach charm using round-nose pliers. Attach 6mm nailheads to tag. Attach rhinestones with glue dots. Attach tag to card.

Happy Birthday Title
by Delores Frantz

MATERIALS: Black cardstock • *EK Success* dotted letter template • 36 assorted *Jewel-Craft* 10mm rhinestones • ¼" circle punch • Craft knife • Mini glue dot

TIPS: Trace and cut out letters. Use punch to cut centers of letters.

Rhinestones & Jewels

Rhinestone and jewels embellish borders, shape flowers and accent letters in this treasure chest of ideas!

Angel
Star
Patterns

Angel *by Valoree Albert*

MATERIALS: Cardstock (Gray, Light Blue, Lavender) • Star print paper • *Scrap Pagerz* party lettering templates • *JewelCraft* (Silver eyelets- -2 large, 4 small; Round Crystal rhinestones - 15mm, two 6mm, three 4mm) • 26 gauge Tinned Copper wire • Star template • Silver cord • Eyelet setter

TIPS: Trace and cut letters from Light Blue cardstock using lettering template. Mount on Lavender and trim leaving thin border. Place at top of page. Accent 'A' with cord. Cut stars from Light Blue and mount on Gray. Trim leaving a thin border. Set eyelets through center of stars. Place swirled wire in center of eyelets and mount on left side. Mount photo on Gray and Lavender. Trim Lavender leaving 1" on right side, mount on Light Blue and place on page. Accent photo mat with rhinestones. Tear Gray cardstock and place on right. Set eyelets at top and bottom of torn cardstock. Thread with cord.

Flower Border
by Delores Frantz

MATERIALS: Cardstock (Pale Green, Dark Purple) • *JewelCraft* (Navette rhinestones - 14 Amber, 14 Amethyst, 4 Green; 4 Gold 4mm filigree nailheads) • ⅝" sheer Green ribbon • Stamp scissors • Mini glue dots

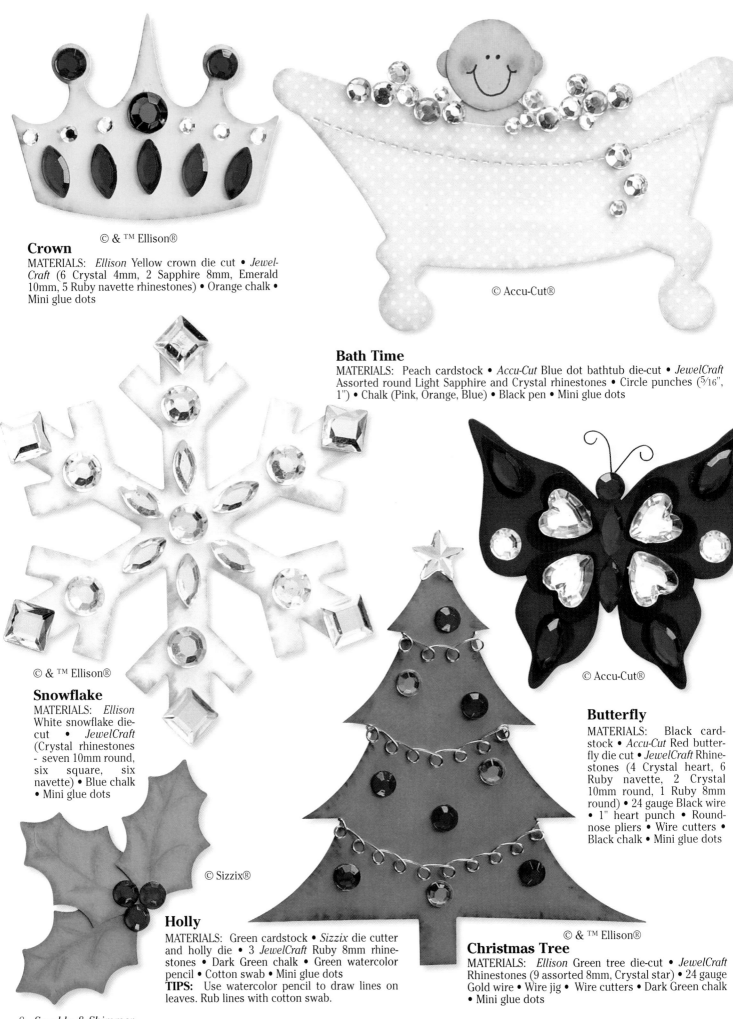

Crown
© & ™ Ellison®
MATERIALS: *Ellison* Yellow crown die cut • *Jewel-Craft* (6 Crystal 4mm, 2 Sapphire 8mm, Emerald 10mm, 5 Ruby navette rhinestones) • Orange chalk • Mini glue dots

© Accu-Cut®

Bath Time
MATERIALS: Peach cardstock • *Accu-Cut* Blue dot bathtub die-cut • *JewelCraft* Assorted round Light Sapphire and Crystal rhinestones • Circle punches (5/16", 1") • Chalk (Pink, Orange, Blue) • Black pen • Mini glue dots

© & ™ Ellison®

Snowflake
MATERIALS: *Ellison* White snowflake die-cut • *JewelCraft* (Crystal rhinestones - seven 10mm round, six square, six navette) • Blue chalk • Mini glue dots

© Accu-Cut®

Butterfly
MATERIALS: Black cardstock • *Accu-Cut* Red butterfly die cut • *JewelCraft* Rhinestones (4 Crystal heart, 6 Ruby navette, 2 Crystal 10mm round, 1 Ruby 8mm round) • 24 gauge Black wire • 1" heart punch • Round-nose pliers • Wire cutters • Black chalk • Mini glue dots

© Sizzix®

Holly
MATERIALS: Green cardstock • *Sizzix* die cutter and holly die • 3 *JewelCraft* Ruby 8mm rhinestones • Dark Green chalk • Green watercolor pencil • Cotton swab • Mini glue dots
TIPS: Use watercolor pencil to draw lines on leaves. Rub lines with cotton swab.

© & ™ Ellison®

Christmas Tree
MATERIALS: *Ellison* Green tree die-cut • *JewelCraft* Rhinestones (9 assorted 8mm, Crystal star) • 24 gauge Gold wire • Wire jig • Wire cutters • Dark Green chalk • Mini glue dots

Love Title
MATERIALS: Cardstock (Deep Red, Black) • Mirror paper • *JewelCraft* Rhinestones (12 Crystal navette, Ruby heart) • 1¼" heart punch • Stamp scissors • Mini glue dots

© & ™ Ellison®

Easter Egg
MATERIALS: Ellison Pink egg die-cut • *Jewel-Craft* Rhinestones (6 Teal navette, 4 Pink navette, 5 Amethyst 4mm round) • Pink chalk • 24 gauge Aqua wire • Wire jig • Wire cutters • Mini glue dots • Tape
TIPS: Place straight line of pegs on jig. Loop wire around pegs leaving ½" tail at each end. Position wire loops on egg. Fold wire tails to back and secure with tape or glue.

Die Cuts
by Delores Frantz

'To die for' die cuts are yours with a few jewels and rhinestones, wire and a lot of imagination!

Add sparkle and shimmer with rhinestones and jewels!

© & ™ Ellison®

Eyeglasses
MATERIALS: *Ellison* Black eyeglasses die-cut • *JewelCraft* (4mm round rhinestones - 6 Peridot, 3 Light Amethyst, 3 Rose, 3 Sapphire, 3 Light Sapphire, 2 Topaz; 4 Peridot navette rhinestones) • Mini glue dots

Ring
MATERIALS: *Ellison* Gold ring die-cut • 4 *JewelCraft Crystal square* rhinestones • Mini glue dots

Sun
MATERIALS: Cardstock (Black, Orange, Red) • *Ellison* Yellow sun die-cut • *JewelCraft* Rhinestones (6 Crystal triangle, 6 Yellow navette) • Punches (⅛" circle, ⅜" heart) • Orange chalk • Black pen • Mini glue dots

© & ™ Ellison®

© & ™ Ellison®

Summer Afternoon
by Deb Ringquist

MATERIALS: *DMD* cardstock (3" x 11" piece of Light Yellow, 3½" x 11½" piece of Light Blue) • *Karen Foster* Island Sunset paper • *Provo Craft* summer afternoon stickers • 8 *Forster* craft sticks • *JewelCraft* (Size 20 round rhinestones - Topaz, Light Sapphire, Emerald, Peridot; Mirrors - 3 diamond 25mm x 11mm round; 6mm spiral nailhead; Gold Metallic Iris sequins-by-the-yard; 4 Baby Blue eyelets) • Eyelet setter • 12" paper trimmer • Hermafix • *Glue dots*

TIPS: Stack cardstock pieces and attach to paper with eyelets. Crop photos, glue on page. Attach craft stick frames and rhinestones to craft sticks with glue dots. Make 'Summer Afternoon' title box and mat with cardstock. Attach round mirror with a glue dot in upper right corner. Bend nailhead prongs in and attach it to mirror. Attach sequins and mirrors using glue dots.

Fish with Sequins
by Stephanie Barnard

MATERIALS: Orange fish die-cut • *JewelCraft* Sequins (Violet, Green Metallic Iris, Gold Metallic Iris) • Glue dot

TIPS: Outline fish with sequins. Fill with rows as shown.

Ocean Page
by Julianna Hudgins

MATERIALS: Cardstock (Cream, Green) • *Design Originals* Water & Swirls paper • Vellum • Border stamp • *Radiant Pearls* Gold ink pad • Die-cuts (Blue fish, Tan starfish) • *JewelCraft* (Silver filigree nailheads - two 8mm, five 6mm, two 4mm; 3 Peridot 6mm rhinestones; Three 9mm mirrors; Green Metallic Iris sequins-by-the-yard; 2 Caviar Bead dolphin appliques) • 24 gauge wire (Lemon, Aqua) • Acrylic metallic paint (Green, Gold, Turquoise) • Sponge • Glue dots

TIPS: Tear vellum for bottom of page, attach with nailheads. Sponge Cream cardstock with paint and stamp with Gold border. Make seaweed with sequins, attach with glue dots. Spiral wire and attach to fish die cut. Cut fish from print paper. Attach remaining accents as shown.

Taylor Page *by Valoree Albert*

MATERIALS: Cardstock (Teal, Yellow) • *Design Originals* vellum • *Creative Imaginations* Bryce & Madeline print paper (Blue, Orange, Yellow, Pink, Green) • *Sizzix* die cutter and flower dies • *JewelCraft* (15mm Topaz rhinestone; Gold Metallic Iris sequins-by-the-yard; Eyelets - 2 Teal, 4 Green) • Eyelet setter • *EK Success* pom-pom punch • *Deja Views* Spunky lettering template • Craft knife

TIPS: Cut letters from Blue paper using template, mount on Yellow cardstock. Tear Teal cardstock for border and mount on top of page. Add title. Set Teal eyelets in White punched flowers in center of letters. Tear Teal cardstock on one side, place on bottom of page. Die cut 4 flowers from print paper. Place 2 flowers under vellum. Secure vellum by setting Green eyelets in each corner. Make flowers. Accent centers of flowers with rhinestones and sequins.

Party Page   *by Valoree Albert*

MATERIALS: *Renae Lindgren* (Yellow and Purple print paper, title, border strip, donkey, flower and frame die-cuts) • *JewelCraft* (Navette rhinestones - Jonquil, Light Sapphire, Rose, Light Amethyst, 2 Peridot; 3 Rose 6mm rhinestones; Mirrors - two 6mm square, 13mm triangle, 25m x 11mm diamond; Nailheads - 4 Silver 6mm spiral, 4mm Silver; Green Metallic Iris sequins-by-the-yard; Pink and Purple FabricPuff flower appliques; Purple bugle beads; Pink and Purple seed beads) • 28 gauge Purple wire • Round-nose pliers

TIPS: Mount 'PARTY' on Purple cardstock. Place border strip along top of page and line with sequins. Mount diamond mirror on Purple, trim and place in center of sequins. Scatter navette rhinestones and square mirrors in top section. Hang donkey from the border and accent with triangle mirror, beaded wire, 4mm nailhead and flower. Accent frame with round rhinestones. Mount White journaling on Purple, trim and secure to page with nailheads. Accent flower punch out with flower applique.

Sequins

From simple strands to elaborately filled shapes, sequins sparkle and shimmer!

Easter Page
by Erin Terrell

MATERIALS: Cardstock (Green, Light Green, Pink, Yellow, Lavender) • *Keeping Memories Alive* Pink linen paper • *Coluzzle* oval template • *SEI* White and Purple letter stickers • *JewelCraft* Iris Sequins - Pink, Yellow, Clear; Green Metallic sequins-by-the-yard; Seed beads - Pink, Green, Yellow) • Craft knife • Needle and thread • Foam mounting squares

TIP: Sew loose sequins and beads on eggs.

Queen of Everything   *by Valoree Albert*

MATERIALS: Cardstock (Navy, Yellow, White) • *Mary Engelbreit©* print paper, die-cuts and stickers • *JewelCraft* (11 assorted rhinestones; 5 square 6mm mirrors; Black Metallic Iris sequins-by-the-yard) • 7/8" Blue sheer ribbon • Black fine tip pen• Pop dots

TIPS: Trim print paper and place at top of page. Place border sticker along bottom edge. Place sequins along 'It's good to be queen' section of print paper. Trim ribbon and place on right side. Mount 'Queen of Everything' on Navy paper, trim and mount over ribbon. Mount photos on Yellow and Navy cardstock. Accent with rhinestones. Mount journaling on Navy and place on page. Accent with stickers and rhinestones. Trim Red cardstock and place along bottom edge. Place queen sticker on bottom. Accent background with mirrors.

'Goldie' Fish *by Stephanie Barnard*
MATERIALS: Orange fish die-cut • *JewelCraft* Rhinestones (Amethyst 6mm, Topaz, 2 Peridot, 2 Sapphire, Light Sapphire, 2 Amethyst and 2 Ruby 4mm) • Glue dots

Angel Collar Pattern

Angel Wing Pattern

Fold

Add a Lark's Head Knot to Each Tag with Paper Twist

Seychelles Tag Pattern

Seychelles *by Carolyn Holt*
MATERIALS: Cardstock (Black, Gold, Blue, Dark Red) • Rubber stamps (*Stephanie Olin* palm tree, *Impress* assorted designs) • Three 1¾" squares of matboard • 10 small tags • Ink pads (Mango Freeze, Summer Sun, Maraschino, Black pigment) • Black embossing powder • *Radiant Pearls* (Sapphire on Ice, Peacock, Royal Gold) • Rust paper twist • *JewelCraft* Assorted seed and bugle beads; 4 small Gold charms; Metallic Iris sequins-by-the-yard - Red, Blue) • Assorted fibers • 26 gauge Black wire • Deckle scissors • Heat gun
TIPS: Stamp and emboss cut out palm tree. Paint palm tree, squares and tags with ink pads. Wrap fibers, beaded wire and sequins around squares. Stamp tags and Blue cardstock. Arrange page as shown.

Memories Card *by Beverley Morgan*
MATERIALS: *DMD* cardstock (6¼" x 7" piece of Aqua, 4" x 7" piece of Denim, 3½" x 5" piece of Orchid) • *Art Impressions* 'Memories' rubber stamp • *Color Box* Purple pigment ink pad • *JewelCraft* (2 Gold 8mm filigree nailheads; 2 Black 4mm faceted beads; Teal seed beads; Blue Metallic Iris sequins-by-the-yard; Large sequin flower applique) • 24 gauge Seafoam Green wire • Wire cutters • Round-nose pliers • Push pin • Craft stick • Mouse pad • *Gem-Tac* adhesive
TIPS: Make 1¾" fold on left side of Aqua cardstock. Attach Orchid to center of Denim. Center and stamp 'Memories' on Aqua fold. With push pin make a hole at each end of Aqua fold near stamped word. Cut 12" of wire. Place one end of wire through top hole and press flat on back. Make flat coil with round-nose pliers to secure. Coil, twist and add beads then attach other end of wire. Place Denim and Orchid cardstock under Aqua fold and mouse pad under Denim. Attach nailheads through layers. Attach sequins and flower.

Angel *by Delores Frantz*

MATERIALS: Cardstock (Metallic Gold, Peach, Blue) • 36" of Gold Metallic Irissequins-by-the-yard • 7 Blue 5mm sequins • 24" of Yellow fiber • Circle punches (1½", 1¼", 1") • Jumbo scallop scissors • Pink chalk • Black pen • Sheet adhesive

TIPS: For halo, punch 1" circle in Gold cardstock. Center a 1¼" circle punch over 1" hole and punch. Glue sequins-by-the-yard on halo. Apply sheet adhesive to right side of Gold cardstock. Cut wings. Press sequins-by-the-yard on adhesive. Wrap fiber around a 3½" square of cardboard. Remove and tie in 3 places with thread. Glue on head.

Scatter, fill and wrap… sequins add luxurious texture and gleaming color to pages and cards.

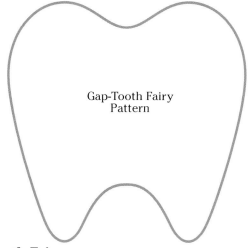

Gap-Tooth Fairy   *by Shannon Landen*

MATERIALS: Cardstock (Lavender print, White) • *Frances Meyer* Pink paper • *JewelCraft* (Silver Metallic Iris sequins-by-the-yard; 10 assorted Crystal and Lavender rhinestones) • *Scrap Pagerz* lettering template • 4 White buttons • White embroidery floss • Tulle • Needle • *American Crafts* Galaxy Marker • Glue dots

TIPS: Using Pink paper and Lavender cardstock, color block background. Attach sequins across center with glue dots. Cut rectangular piece of tulle. Tie knots at each corner. Place picture in rectangle and adhere to page. Sew floss through button holes, tie knots and glue buttons on tulle. Sprinkle sequins on tulle and glue in place. Place rhinestones on page, working them into paper pattern. Using lettering template, trace title on page with marker.

Waves Border   *by Delores Frantz*

MATERIALS: Blue cardstock • Blue Metallic Iris sequins-by-the-yard • Toothpick • Thick White glue

TIPS: Transfer waves to cardstock. Use toothpick to place thin line of glue along curved lines. Press 4" pieces of sequins-by-the-yard into glue.

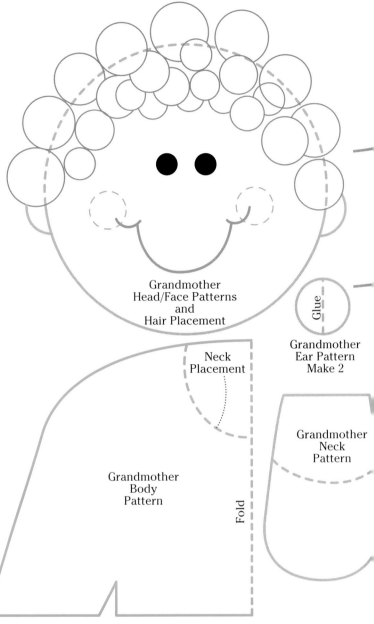

Grandmother
Head/Face Patterns
and
Hair Placement

Glue

Grandmother
Ear Pattern
Make 2

Neck
Placement

Grandmother
Body
Pattern

Fold

Grandmother
Neck
Pattern

Grandmother *by Delores Frantz*

MATERIALS: Cardstock (Black, Navy Blue, Medium Blue, Rust, Peach) • Gold flower paper • *JewelCraft* (Gold charms - triple heart, 7 hearts, 6 flowers; Seed beads - Pearl, Blue, Dark Blue) • Wire (24 gauge Dark Brown, 26 gauge Dark Blue) • Beading needle and thread • Circle punches ($\frac{1}{8}$", $\frac{3}{4}$", 3") • Wire cutters • Round-nose pliers • Chalk (Pink, Orange) • Red pen • Mini glue dots • Glue

TIPS: Make nine $\frac{5}{8}$", eight $\frac{1}{2}$" and seven $\frac{3}{8}$" coils of Dark Brown wire with $\frac{1}{2}$" tails. Punch holes in head with pin and insert wire tails from front to back. Bend wire tail tightly against back of head. Secure with glue. Thread beads and charms on wire. Charms may be left loose or secured with glue dots.

Tag Pattern

The Errigo Boys *by Valoree Albert*

MATERIALS: Cardstock (Sage, Light Blue, Ivory) • *Mary Engelbreit*© Black and Blue print paper and leaf stickers • Funky Town beads • *JewelCraft* (Large and small Silver eyelets; Silver heart charm) • 26 gauge Bare Copper wire • Green fiber • *Provo Craft* block lettering template • Craft knife

TIPS: Cut letters from Black paper, mount on Ivory and trim. Hand write 'The' and 'Boys' and cut from Ivory cardstock with craft knife. Place title at top of page. Tear strips of Sage and Light Blue cardstock. Center Blue paper near bottom of page. Place torn strips at top and bottom of Blue. Set eyelets on each side of page at bottom. Thread beads on wire, place heart charm in center and finish threading beads. Place wire through eyelets and secure on back. Mount photo on Ivory, Black paper and Ivory. Write journaling on vellum and place on tag. Set eyelet at top of tag and thread fibers through eyelet. Thread beads on wire and accent the top of tag. Secure vellum with leaf stickers. Place border stickers at top and bottom of page.

Best Friends Hand
Pattern
Make 2 -
Reverse 1

Kristy and Jan have
been best friends
since the 4th grade

Best Friends *by Delores Frantz*
MATERIALS: Cardstock (Peach, Deep Red, White, Silver, Gold) • Denim paper • *JewelCraft* (6 Silver and 6 Gold charms) • Chain (2½" of Silver, 2½" of Gold) • 4mm jump rings (5 Silver, 5 Gold) • Stamp scissors • *Sizzix* Die-cutter and alphabet dies • Needle and thread • Orange chalk • Mini glue dots
Tips: Attach charms to chain with jump rings. Sew ends of chain to paper.

Charms

Charms are the perfect addition for borders or ornament trims… try them dozens of ways!

Kristy & Carla
Christmas 2000

Happy Holiday
Ornament Patterns

Happy Holiday *by Delores Frantz*
MATERIALS: Cardstock (White, Deep Red, Moss Green, Metallic Gold) • *Design Originals* Green Scrappin' paper • *JewelCraft* (33 assorted Gold and Silver charms; Metallic Iris sequins-by-the-yard - 6" of Red, 9" of Green) • 15" of Gold thread • 26 gauge Gold wire • Wire cutters • Round-nose pliers • Scissors (jumbo scallop, stamp) • Circle punches (5/16", ½", 3") • *Sizzix* Die-cutter and alphabet dies • Mini glue dots
TIPS: Make the wire dangles or thread charms on wire. Print journaling.

Bear Card *by JewelCraft*

MATERIALS: 5½" x 6" Gold card • Cardstock (Cream, Dark Red, Black) • *JewelCraft* (Caviar Bead teddy bear applique; 2 Gold 4mm nailheads) • Black fine tip pen

TIPS: Cut Black strip for center of card. Tear Dark Red square and attach applique. Attach to strip. Write message and attach with nailheads.

Sunflower Card *by Lauren Johnston*

MATERIALS: Cardstock (5½" x 11" piece and 2¾" square of Black, 5⅛" and 2¼" squares of Cream) • Large sunflower rubber stamp • *Ancient Page* Sienna dye ink pad • *Color Box* Brown pigment ink pad • Copper embossing powder • Piece of Fun Foam • Cork from wine bottle • *JewelCraft* 12 Gold 6mm nailheads • Stud setter • Heat gun • *Marvy* Brilliant Yellow marker • Double-sided foam tape • Double-stick tape

TIPS: Stamp single Sienna sunflower on 2¾" Cream square, glue on Black square. Color petals Yellow. Stamp Sienna sunflower 8 times on 5⅛" Cream square. Color petals Yellow. To emboss nailheads, insert prongs in top or side of cork and dab with pigment ink. Sprinkle with embossing powder and heat. Let studs cool completely before removing from cork. Place stamped piece on Fun Foam and pierce card with stud. Secure on back with setter tool. Fill center with embossed studs. Apply small pieces of foam tape to back avoiding studded area. Fold remaining Black cardstock in half for card. Attach large sunflower square and Black square with double stick tape. Add a small sunflower square.

Beads & Clay Tag *by Beverley Morgan*

MATERIALS: *DMD* cardstock (2¾" x 4½" piece of Tan, 3" x 5" piece of Clay) • *Hero Arts* garden design III rubber stamp • *Color Box* pigment ink pads (Sea Grass, Bare Copper) • Translucent *Sculpey Premo* clay • *JewelCraft* (Gold 6mm spiral nailhead; Blue mix bugle beads) • 24 gauge Peacock Blue wire • *Simply Plaid* letter stencil • ¼" hole punch • Wire cutters • Round-nose pliers • Small sponge applicator • Push pin • Clay cutting blade • Glue dots

TIPS: Prepare one section of clay following manufacturer's instructions. Roll to ⅛" thick. Stamp with garden design and cut 2" square with blade. Pierce hole in each corner. Press nailhead in center and bake. Cut ⅝" off top corners of cardstock pieces. Punch hole ¼" down from top of Clay cardstock. Align Tan cardstock ⅛" from bottom of Clay, attach with glue dots. Cut three 4" and one 10" pieces of wire. Using round-nose pliers, form loop at one end of 4" wires, roll loop 3 to 4 turns with fingers to spiral. Thread beads and insert wires in clay, bend wire to lie flat. Fold 10" wire in half, insert in tag and lace ends through loop and form lark's head knot. Add beads and shape as shown. Place stencil on upper half of tag, apply Copper ink with applicator. Attach Clay piece in center of tag with glue dots.

Star Card Pattern

Star Card *by Lauren Johnston*

MATERIALS: Cardstock (4¼" square of Royal Blue, 4¾" square of Red) • 5" x 6½" White card • Star rubber stamp • Blue ink pad • 30 *JewelCraft* Silver star nailheads • Stud setter • Piece of Fun Foam • Scissors • White chalk pencil • Red marker • Double-sided foam tape • Double-stick tape

TIPS: Using chalk pencil, draw very lightly around star pattern on Royal Blue. Insert studs along pattern lines. Place card on Fun Foam and pierce card with stud. Secure on back with setter tool. Apply small pieces of foam tape to entire back avoiding studded areas. Attach Blue star piece to Red. Determine placement on front of card but do not attach. Stamp stars around area that will not be covered. Fill empty spaces with Red dots. Attach layers with double stick tape.

'Shades' Card
by Lauren Johnston

MATERIALS: Cardstock (3" x 5" piece of Black, 1⅝" x 3¾" piece of Red, Glossy White) • Mirror paper • *Stampworks* sunglasses rubber stamp • Ancient Page Coal dye ink pad • *JewelCraft* Nailheads (12 Silver 6mm flat, 26 Silver mini) • Piece of Fun Foam • Stud setter • Craft knife • Black Peel n Stick foam squares • Double-stick tape • Double-sided foam tape

TIPS: Stamp sunglasses on White cardstock. Insert studs on top rim of glasses. Place stamped piece on foam, pierce card with studs. Secure on back with setter. Cut out sunglasses and around inside glass portion with craft knife. Cut pieces of mirror paper slightly larger than inside openings, apply to back with tape. Apply small pieces of foam tape to entire back avoiding studded area. Attach to Red and Black cardstock. Attach studs around edge.

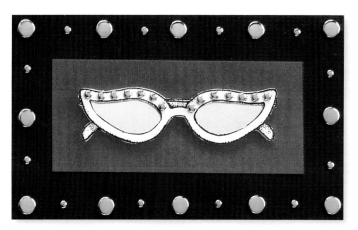

Nailheads

Accent the die-cuts, add borders and attach photo frames with metallic nailheads.

Jazz up anything using metal nailheads!

Ladybug Card *by JewelCraft*

MATERIALS: Cardstock (4¼" x 11" Red card, 3 Red 2½" squares, 3 Black 2⅝" squares) • *JewelCraft* (3 Caviar Bead ladybug appliques; 12 Silver 4mm nailheads) • Black fine tip pen

TIPS: Attach ladybugs to Red squares and Red squares to Black. Attach nailheads to corners. Attach to card. Draw border with pen.

American Pride *by Valoree Albert*

MATERIALS: *DMD* cardstock (Navy, Natural) • *Design Originals* print paper (Gold Stars on Ivory, Stars and Stripes) • *Li'l Davis Designs* eagle laser cut • *EK Success* varsity lettering template • *JewelCraft* (9 Nickel 4mm flat nailheads; Caviar Bead US flag star appliques) • Craft knife

TIPS: Tear Navy cardstock and place at top of Ivory paper. Tear Natural cardstock along one edge and mount on Navy leaving ½" at top. Set nailheads along top of page. Cut letters from stars and stripes paper, mount on torn Natural cardstock. Hand write 'pride' under title. Mount photos on Natural and Navy. Tear Natural cardstock for journaling and mount on Navy. Accent top of journaling with star appliques. Assemble laser cut to create Uncle Sam eagle and place on page.

Heart Card   by Lauren Johnston
MATERIALS: Cardstock (White Glossy, Gold Glossy) • Vellum • Heart rubber stamp • *ColorBox* Frost White pigment ink pad • White embossing powder • *JewelCraft* Large and small Gold heart nailheads • Piece of Fun Foam • Stud setter • Heat gun • Double-sided foam tape • Double-stick tape

TIPS: Stamp heart on vellum and emboss. Cut vellum in a rectangle slightly larger than stamped image. Cut Gold cardstock slightly larger than vellum. Center vellum over Gold cardstock and insert small heart nailheads at each corner. Place card on fun foam, pierce with nailhead where desired and secure on back with setter. Apply small pieces of double-sided foam tape to the entire back avoiding prong areas. Cut White cardstock slightly larger than Gold piece, attach. Attach 3 layers to front of 4¼" x 5" card with double-stick tape. Insert large heart nailheads making sure prongs go through heavier paper. Cover the inside of the card with White cardstock, attach with double stick tape.

Lighthouse   by Deb Ringquist
MATERIALS: *DMD* cardstock (Light Denim, Jute) • *Li'l Davis* shell die-cuts (Green, Tan, Cream) • Out West beads • Shell charms (4 Gold, 3 Silver) • Starfish charms (4 Silver, 3 Gold) • White fiber • 8 White eyelets • Eyelet setter • Wire cutters • Fiskars 12" paper trimmer • *Gem-Tac* adhesive • Glue dots • *Hermafix*

TIPS: Tear 3 Jute strips to make sand, glue on Light Denim with Hermafix. Spread a thin coat of Gem-Tac on top of torn cardstock. Place beads on glue and let dry. Cut loops off charms with wire cutters. Attach charms and die cuts to sand with glue dots. Tear Jute to make frames and set frames with eyelets after pictures are attached with Hermafix. Cut Jute cardstock tag by hand and attach cropped picture of lighthouse sign with Hermafix. Tie fiber bows and attach with Gem-Tac.

Mini Flower Card
by Lauren Johnston
MATERIALS: Cardstock (White, Gold Glossy) • 3" square White envelope • *Impress* mini flower rubber stamp • *Color Box* Gold pigment • Gold embossing powder • *JewelCraft* (4mm Gold nailhead; 4mm Crystal rhinestone) • Piece of Fun Foam • Stud setter • Heat gun • Double-sided foam tape • Double-stick tape • *Gem-Tac* adhesive

TIPS: Glue a rhinestone in center of nailhead, let dry. On White cardstock, stamp single flower with Gold ink and emboss with Gold powder. Trim close to edges. Insert rhinestone nailhead in center of flower by placing stamped piece on foam and piercing card with prongs. Secure on back with setter. Place pieces of foam tape on stamped flower square avoiding prongs. Cut 3" x 6" piece of White cardstock and fold in half. Cut Gold cardstock slightly larger than stamped piece. Cut White slightly larger and one more piece of Gold slightly larger. Layer pieces and secure with double stick tape. Stamp matching envelope.

Valentine's   by Shannon Landen
MATERIALS: Cardstock (Red/Gold fleck, Tan, Black) • *Metropolis* Metallic Gold paper • *JewelCraft* Gold sequins; Black and Gold seed and bugle beads; 4 Black eyelets) • Eyelet setter • White tulle • 26 gauge Gold wire • *Inspire Graphics* cursive font • *Scotch* photo mending tape • *Tombow* Mono Multi liquid glue • Glue dots

TIPS: Wrap beads in tulle. String beads randomly on wire and wrap wire around tulle. Secure wire and tulle on back.

Africa *by Carolyn Holt*

MATERIALS: Cardstock (Rust, Green, White) • Brown print paper • Small vellum envelope • Rubber stamps (*PSX* compass and passport, *Impress Me* primitive designs, *A Stamp in the Hand* corner) • Ink pads (Rust, White, Clear embossing , Brown) • Embossing powder (Gold, Rust) • 2 postage stamps • *Radiant Pearls* (Summer Sun, Autumn Leaf, Royal Gold, Fandango Green, Olive Branch) • 6 assorted *JewelCraft* Gold nailheads • Assorted fibers • Key on small ring

TIPS: Stamp Green and White cardstock as shown. Stamp and emboss corners and compass, cut out. Stamp passport, cut out. Paint background and mats with Radiant Pearls.

Nailheads

Tag Pattern

Tag or Card *by Beverley Morgan*

MATERIALS: 8½" x 11" piece of DMD Tan cardstock • *Rubber Stampede* tribal frame rubber stamp • *Color Box* Copper pigment ink pad • 30mm x 40mm mirror • 24 gauge Purple wire • *JewelCraft* (4 Gold 6mm nailheads; Multi mix beads - faceted, seed; 4 Emerald 4mm rhinestones) • Translucent *Sculpey Premo* clay • *Simply Plaid* laser template • Clay cutting blade • ¼" hole punch • Wire cutters • Round-nose pliers • Small sponge applicator • *Gem-Tac* • Pop dots

TIPS: Prepare one section of clay following manufacturer's instructions. Roll to ⅛". Stamp clay with tribal frame. Cut 2" square around design with clay blade. Press nailheads in corners and bake. Cool. Glue rhinestones on corners and mirror in center. Cut 3" x 5" piece of cardstock. Cut ⅝" off top corners and set aside. Punch hole ¼" down from top center. Cut 14" and 12" pieces of wire. Using pliers form a small loop at one end of 12" piece, roll loop with fingers 3 to 4 turns to form coil. Thread seed beads on wire and make coil at end. Place stencil on the upper half of tag and apply Copper ink with a small sponge applicator. Attach clay piece in center of tag with pop dots. Form 12" beaded wire around clay piece and up to left side of tag. Attach wire with Gem-Tac. Thread faceted beads on 14" wire leaving only enough space for a small loop at each end. Place wire through hole in cardstock, twist one time then coil each ends with fingers.

Carl Ohm *by Carolyn Holt*

MATERIALS: Tan cardstock • Paper (*K & Company* Black stripe, *Scrap Ease* marble) • Rubber stamps (*PSX, Stampers Anonymous*) • Black ink pads • Gold *Radiant Pearls* • Letter tiles • *A Lost Art* heart charm • 18 Gold 4mm *JewelCraft* nailheads • White/Gold tassel • Seed and bugle beads • *Gem-Tac*

TIPS: Stamp stripe background paper with travel designs. Paint mat paper with radiant Pearls. Attach photos and mats to background with nailheads.

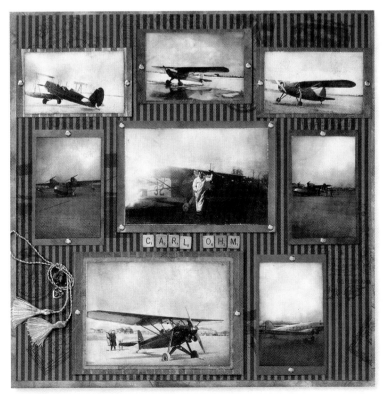

Fireworks Pattern

America the Beautiful *by Valoree Albert*

MATERIALS: *DMD* cardstock (Navy, Natural) • *Design Originals* print paper (Gold stars on Ivory, Stars and Stripes) • *JewelCraft* (Pearl Gold nailheads - four 4mm, two 6mm; 4mm round rhinestones - Ruby, Sapphire, Crystal; FabricPuff Blue star applique; Freedom beads) • Wire (26 gauge Blue, 24 gauge Red, 22 gauge Tinned Copper) • Round-nose pliers • Black fine tip pen

TIPS: Trim Navy cardstock to 11" square and place in center of stars on Gold paper. Trim stars and stripes paper and place 2" from top of page. Trim Natural cardstock for title and secure with 6mm nailheads. Shape 'America' with Blue wire and pliers. Form Red wire spiral and place over 'I'. Hand write 'the beautiful' and mount photo on Natural and stars and stripes, accent with star fabric puff. Make fireworks with Blue, Red and Silver wire. Thread beads on wire and place rhinestone in center of each burst. String beads on 22 gauge wire and coil, secure with nailheads. Trim Natural cardstock for journaling and secure with nailheads.

Mommy & Me *by Shannon Landen*

MATERIALS: Cardstock (Yellow, Pink) • *Mary Englebreit*© Yellow print paper • Silver Pearl embossing powder • Ribbon (¼" sheer Pink, ¾" sheer White, ⅜" Yellow, ⅜" Pink) • *JewelCraft* (FabricPuff White flower border applique; Rhinestones -6 assorted 8mm, Jonquil heart; Yellow Iris sequins; Beads - Healing, True Love) • 1¾" White eyelet lace • Silver heart charm • 28 gauge White wire • Wendy medium font • Embossing pen • Craft knife • Glue dots • Spray adhesive • Tombo Mono Multi liquid glue

TIPS: Glue trims on page and rhinestones on centers of lace flowers. Thread beads on wire and shape into heart. Tie bow with ¾" ribbon and glue sequin to center. Thread sheer Pink ribbon through charm and tie to side of wire heart. Print words on Pink cardstock, emboss and cut out. Finish as shown.

Heart Pattern

Christmas Lights Border *by Delores Frant*

MATERIALS: 24 gauge wire (Gold, Black) • Seed beads (Blue, Lavender, Pale Yellow, Pale Green, Rose) • Wire cutters • Round-nose pliers • ¼" dowel

TIPS: Thread one color of seed beads on Black wire. Twist wire together leaving a short and a long tail. Shape light. Wrap Gold wire around dowel to make coiled base. Thread base on Black wire and push against beads. Glue to secure. Continue making lights leaving 4" or 5" of wire between lights.

Flower Border *by Delores Frantz*

MATERIALS: Cardstock (Yellow, Green, Red) • *JewelCraft* (7 Green 4mm rhinestones; Pale Green and Red seed beads) • 26 gauge Kelly Green wire • Flower punches (5/16", 1") • Wire cutters • Stamp, scissors • Mini glue dots

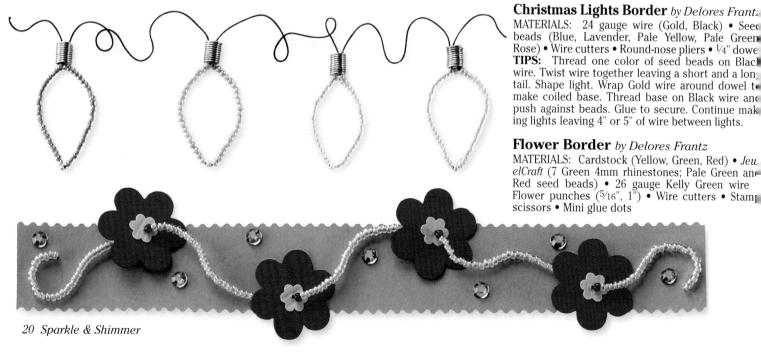

My Heart *by Valoree Albert*

MATERIALS: Cardstock (Red, White, Black) • Red dot print paper • *JewelCraft* (2 FabricPuff Red gingham heart appliques; Red Hot and True Love beads) • 24 gauge Red wire • Round-nose pliers • Computer generated journaling

TIPS: Trim Red cardstock to 11" square, cut out center leaving ½" border and place in center of White. Tear a piece of Black and place at bottom. Trim White and Red and place on Black. Trim smaller piece of White, place on Red and journal. Mount photo on White, print, White and Black. Shape words with wire and accent by placing beads on wire. Use pliers to coil ends. String Red beads on wire and shape into heart. Accent sides of journaling with heart appliques.

Wire & Beads

Thread beads on wire and shape... these designs are wonderful visual treats!

Real Boy *by Valoree Albert*

MATERIALS: Cardstock (Red, White, Natural, Black) • *Mary Engelbreit©* print paper and stickers • 5 Gold *JewelCraft* 4mm nailheads • Heritage beads • 26 gauge Tinned Copper wire • Computer generated journaling

TIPS: Trim Red cardstock and place along right edge of page leaving ⅞" border. Place checkered sticker along edge of Red. Mount photos on White and Black. Place 'To become a real boy' sticker on White and trim edge. Mount on Natural and secure to Red using nailheads. Journal on White and mount on Natural. Trim around the edge and mount. Accent with bead letter and checkered stickers. Secure sword with nailhead. String beads on to wire and coil into swirled pattern, secure with small pieces of wire.

Sarah & Kaitlin *by Shannon Landen*

MATERIALS: Cardstock (2 sheets of Red, White, Navy) • 3 *Paper Patch* star print papers • 11 tiny star charms • Four 12mm square mirrors • Freedom beads • 26 gauge wire (Red, Tinned Copper, Blue) • *Pockets On A Roll* • *Family Treasures* square punches (1¼", ¾") • Needle • Blue pen • *Scotch* photo mending tape • Mini glue dots

TIPS: Layer print paper squares on White cardstock and place along top and left side of Red cardstock background. Color block page using Red and Navy cardstock. Place photo on page with punched squares under corners as shown. String beads and stars on wire leaving 1½" of wire at ends. Twist wires together. With needle, pierce holes next to photo and edge of page. Thread wire ends through holes and tape on back. Write title on pocket with marker and adhere corners with glue dots. Attach mirrors to cover glue dots.

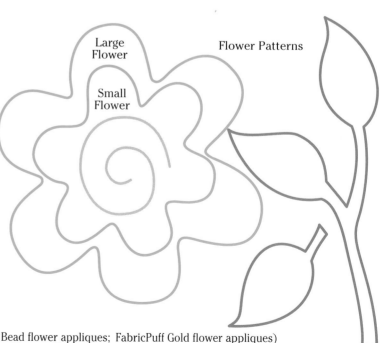

Fly a Kite
by Valoree Albert

MATERIALS: Cardstock (Ivory, White, Black, Yellow) • *Renae Lindgren* print paper, punch outs and stickers • Ocean beads • 4 Gold eyelets • Eyelet setter • Black marker

TIPS: Trim print paper and place on left side of page. Print journaling on White paper, trim and mount on right side. Accent bottom with pinwheel stickers secured with nailheads. Mount large pinwheel and 'Fly a Kite' stickers on White and Black. Print title on White, trim and mount on Black. Place cloud on page and accent with beads. Mount photo on Yellow and Black.

Little Girls
by Valoree Albert

MATERIALS: Cardstock (Teal, White, Ivory) • *Anna Griffin* Ivory print paper • *JewelCraft* FabricPuff Blue and Gold butterfly appliques • Funky Town beads • Wire (24 gauge Turquoise, 26 gauge Dark Blue) • Wire Worker tool with large dowel • Blue and Yellow chalk • Black fine tip pen

TIPS: Trim pieces of patterned paper into thin strips and place on Ivory cardstock. Mount photo on Ivory, White and Teal. Print title on White, color with chalk, trim and mount on Teal. String beads on Dark Blue wire and shape wire into butterfly. Make butterfly body with Peacock wire and wire tool and wings with beaded wire. Attach butterfly appliques and make trails with Dark Blue wire.

FabricPuff appliques create colorful dimension on scrapbook pages.

Flowers Page   *by Valoree Albert*

MATERIALS: Brown Kraft cardstock • *Design Originals* vellum • *Renae Lindgren* print paper (plaid, fabric pieces) • *Sizzix* die-cuts (small White flower, large White flower, Green leaves) • Old West beads • *JewelCraft* (Silver nailheads - ten 4mm flat, two 6mm; Caviar Bead flower appliques; FabricPuff Gold flower appliques) • 28 gauge Tinned Copper wire

TIPS: Place vellum over fabric paper. Trim plaid paper and place at bottom of page. Attach nailheads along top edge. Place die cut flowers and leaves and flower appliques behind plaid paper. Accent center of die cut flowers with beads strung on wire and shaped into spirals. Mount photos on Brown and place on page. Trim Brown, place vellum in center and secure with nailheads for journaling.

Reflection *by Valoree Albert*

MATERIALS: Cardstock (Ivory, Pink) • *Design Originals* print paper (floral on Green, roses & letters) • *JewelCraft* (3 Amethyst heart rhinestones; True Love beads; 40mm x 30mm oval mirror) • 26 gauge Tinned Copper wire • Craft knife • Pink pen

TIPS: Tear Green paper and place along bottom edge of Rose paper. Tear Ivory cardstock and place over Green paper. Hand write 'Reflection', trim with craft knife and mount on Ivory. Write rest of title with Pink marker. Mount photos on Ivory, trim and mount on Green paper. Trim around a section of roses with craft knife and place journaling behind cut out roses. String beads on wire, shape into swirl accents and place on corners of photos. Accent the page with rhinestones.

Corner Design Pattern - Make 2 Reverse 2

ride a bike
have a catch
catch a fish
make mud
play tag
climb a tree
dig some dirt
pick flowers

·TAYLOR·
SUMMER
2000

Wire & Beads

Need photo corners to match a theme? Make them in the colors and shapes you need with beads and wire. Easy!

Add Sparkle with Beads!

Season of Joy

by Valoree Albert

MATERIALS: Cardstock (Stone, Metallic Olive, Hunter Green) • *Design Originals* paper (floral on Green, love letters, vellum) • *JewelCraft* Ruby rhinestones - three 4mm, three 8mm; Red Hot and Old West beads; 4 Gold 3mm flat nailheads) • 26 gauge Tinned Copper wire • Gold thread • Beading thread and needle • Black fine tip pen

TIPS: Trim Stone cardstock and place at top of love letters paper, place nailheads in top corners. String beads on thread and place under Stone. Print title on vellum and place at top of page. Cut oval vellum tag and slip Gold thread through hole at top. Cut holly leaves from Green patterned paper and accent tag and title. Use rhinestones for holly berries. Mount photo on Hunter Green and Olive. String Red beads on thread and accent each corner of photo. String beads on wire and twist into shape, secure on journaling block with nailheads.

Season of Joy Holly Patterns

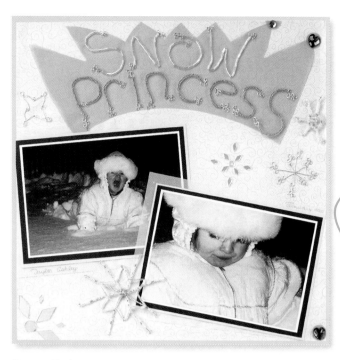

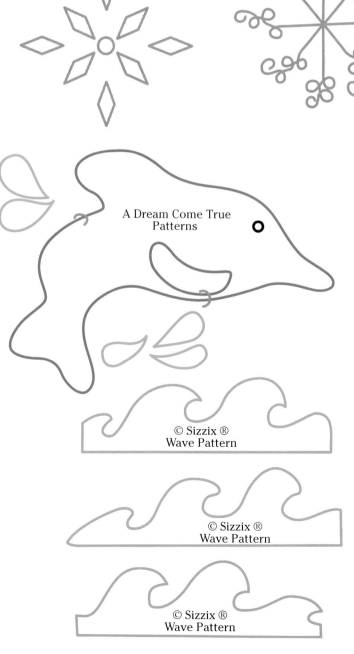

Snow Princess   *by Valoree Albert*

MATERIALS: Cardstock (White, Black) • *Mary Engelbreit*© Blue print paper • Blue & Gold fleck vellum • *JewelCraft* (Aqua 2 rhinestones -2 heart, 8mm; Beads -Ocean, True Love; Mirrors - three 25mm x 11mm diamond, ten 7mm x 3mm diamond, 9mm round; Clear iris sequin) • 26 gauge Tinned Copper wire • ½" circle punch • Round-nose pliers

TIPS: Cut crown from Blue vellum and place at top of page, accent with rhinestones. String beads on wire. Finish ends and shape into letters. Mount letters on crown. Mount photos on White, Black, White and fleck vellum. Create snowflakes with diamond and round mirrors and beads strung on wire.

Snow Princess
Snowflake Patterns

A Dream Come True
Patterns

A Dream Come True   *by Carolyn Grey*

MATERIALS: Cardstock (White, Yellow, Blue, Black) • *JewelCraft* Caviar Bead appliques (3 dolphin, 2 flower) • *Making Memories* Blue paper (print, solid) • Blue seed beads • *Sizzix* wave die-cuts • 26 gauge Powder Blue wire • *EK Success* 1" sun punch • ⅛" hole punch • Needle and thread • *Cock-A-Doodle* Design cursive font • Blue chalk • Black fine tip marker • Pop dots

TIPS: Tear clouds from White cardstock and shade with chalk. Attach die cut waves with pop dots. Hand cut water drops. Outline shapes and White mats with marker. Thread beads on wire and shape dolphin. Sew dolphin on page. Punch Black circle and glue in place for eye.

© Sizzix ®
Wave Pattern

© Sizzix ®
Wave Pattern

© Sizzix ®
Wave Pattern

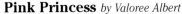

Pink Princess *by Valoree Albert*

MATERIALS: Cardstock (White Pearl, White, Pink, Light Pink) • *JewelCraft* (Pink seed beads; Crystal bugle beads; Two 25mm x 11mm diamond mirrors; 2 Pink 8mm rhinestones; Violet Metallic Iris sequins-by-the-yard; 4 Silver 6mm filigree nailheads; 4 FabricPuff Purple flower appliques) • 26 gauge Tinned Copper wire • Dragonfly cutout • *Creating Keepsakes* pretty font

TIPS: Mount photo on White and Dark Pink cardstock. Print journaling on White Pearl and mount on Pink cardstock. Thread beads on wire and bend to form letters. Use round-nose pliers to make loops in ends. Make tiara using the same technique and curl ends. To make shape at bottom, thread beads on wire leaving extra wire at ends. Loop wire at each end to secure beads. Bend wire by hand to create design.

Snow Princess
and
Let It Snow
Snowflake Pattern

Wire & Beads

Never have titles or snowflakes and other colorful shapes been so filled with interest … wire and beads are it!

Beads Add Glitz and Glamour!

Let It Snow *by Deb Ringquist*

MATERIALS: *DMD* cardstock (Blue, White) • Vellum • *CUT-IT-UP* die-cuts (Snowman with broom, trees, snowflakes, 'Let it Snow') • *JewelCraft* (True love beads; Rhinestones - 2 Crystal 4mm, 4mm Light Sapphire, 20mm Light Sapphire) • *Fiskars* 12" paper trimmer • Green and Blue chalk • *Gem-Tac* adhesive • Mini glue dots • *Hermafix*

TIPS: Cut 12" piece of White cardstock and trim to 5". Tear cardstock toward you. Place on bottom of Blue cardstock for snow. Place Gem-Tac on torn edges and press in beads, let dry. Shade trees with Green chalk and attach to snow with Hermafix. Assemble snowman with glue dots. Place 4mm Crystal rhinestones on Snowman for buttons. Shade 'Let it Snow' title and snowman with Blue chalk. Attach Light Sapphire rhinestones to title. Attach true love beads to vellum snowflakes with Gem-Tac, let dry. Attach snowflakes to page with glue dots. Thread beads on wire, secure ends and form beaded snowflake.

Bride Card *Valoree Albert*

MATERIALS: 4" x 5½" White card • Cardstock (Blue, Blue, Orange, Flesh) • Pearl seed beads • *Jewel-Craft* (Four 7mm x 3mm mirrors; 4mm Crystal rhinestone; FabricPuff White border applique) • White tulle • Gold heart charm • 28 gauge White wire • 1¼" circle punch • Pink chalk • Black fine tip pen • Pop dot

TIPS: Punch face and bangs and cut hair. Punch Blue circle. Glue face and bangs on front of Blue circle. String beads on wire. Attach beads, mirrors and rhinestone for headpiece. Glue tulle behind mirrors. Attach hair to Blue torn cardstock and attach face with pop dot. Thread beads on wire adding charm in center. Finish card as shown.

Make Your Pages Sparkle with Beads!

July 4th   *by Deb Ringquist*

MATERIALS: *DMD* cardstock (Red, Navy, White) • *Design Originals* print paper (large stars on Navy, patriotic flags) • *CUT-IT-UP* die-cuts (Navy July, Red 4, White 'th', Navy heart) • *JewelCraft* (4 Gold 6mm spiral nailheads; Caviar Bead US flag applique; 2 small Gold heart charms; Ruby 14mm heart rhinestone) • 24 gauge Red wire • *Fiskars* 12" paper trimmer • Paper crimper • Mouse pad • *Forster* craft stick • Chalk (Red, White, Blue) • Black marker • *Hermafix* • Glue dots

TIPS: Cut 3" x 10¾" White and 3½" x 11¼" Navy border strips. Place on mouse pad and insert nailheads in corners. Turn border over and bend prongs in with craft stick. Attach July, 4 and flag with glue dots. Chalk 'th' Red, White and Blue, attach. Using Hermafix, attach border to Red. Make journal box with Navy and White. Attach heart to journal with glue dot. Use print papers to mat photo and attach with Hermafix. Cut 12" of Red wire, run through crimper. String heart charms on wire and wrap around Navy heart. Attach the heart with Hermafix.

Be True   *by Valoree Albert*

MATERIALS: Cardstock (White, Red, Navy, Tan, Silver, Dark Red) • *Design Originals* print paper (Gold Stars on Ivory, Gold Stars on Navy, Gold Stars on Burgundy) • Wire (26 gauge Egg White, 26 gauge Tinned Copper, 24 gauge Lemon, 24 gauge Blue, 24 gauge Red) • Silver mylar fringe • Wire Worker with thin dowel • Navy button • Black fine tip pen

TIPS: Trim Ivory paper and place at top of page on Dark Red background. Trim Navy paper, place on left side. Print title on White and mount on Burgundy. Use wire worker to make coil of 26 gauge Egg White wire. Hang title using the coil and button. Make firework burst with wire worker tool and Blue, Red and Egg White wire. Make Uncle Sam and add Egg White wire swirls for beard. Make sparkler with Silver wire using wire worker and thin dowel. Mount photo on Navy and White and accent corners and sparkler with Lemon wire swirls.

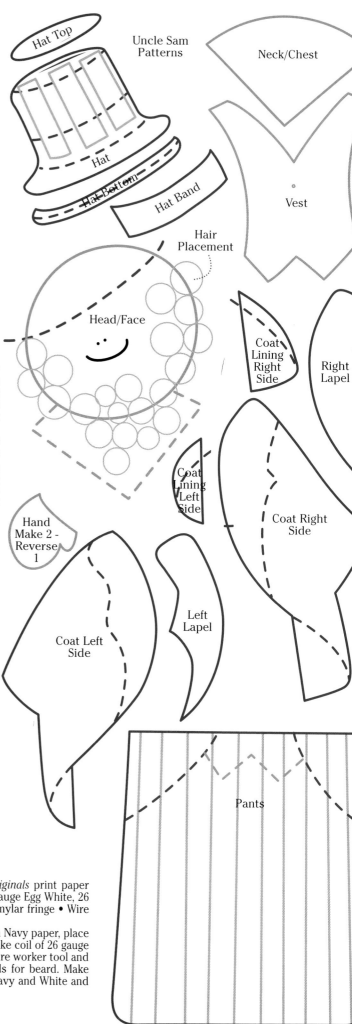

Uncle Sam Patterns

Hat Top

Hat

Hat Bottom

Hat Band

Neck/Chest

Vest

Hair Placement

Head/Face

Coat Lining Right Side

Right Lapel

Coat Lining Left Side

Coat Right Side

Hand Make 2 - Reverse 1

Coat Left Side

Left Lapel

Pants

Boys Will Be Boys *by Erin Terrell*

MATERIALS: Green cardstock • *Provo Craft* print paper (Green squiggles, Green screen) • Vellum • Green letter die-cut • 2 *JewelCraft* Caviar Bead frog appliques • Green letter die-cuts • 24 gauge Green wire • Circle punches (3¼", 3", 1½", 1¼", ⅞", ⅝") • Pink and Yellow chalk • Glue dots • Tape

TIPS: Make Black and White copy of photo, color cheeks Pink and hair Yellow. Mat photo as shown. Punch vellum circles and circles for frames from Green. Frame vellum and add appliques. Make wire swirls, insert ends in page and secure on back with tape.

Crimp Wire

1. Run the wire through a crimper.

2. Wrap around die cut.

Coil Wire

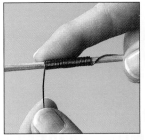

1. Wrap wire around dowel to coil.

2. Pull the ends to stretch the coil.

Spiral Wire

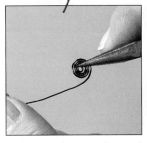
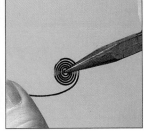

1. Make a loop in the end of the wire.

2. Hold wire with needle-nose pliers and hand shape spiral.

Toad-ally Awesome Kid *by Valoree Albert*

MATERIALS: *Renae Lindgren* cardstock (Green, White, Kraft, Dark Green) • *JewelCraft (*2 Caviar Bead frog appliques; 4 Gold 4mm nailheads; Green Metallic Iris sequins-by-the-yard) • 24 gauge Green wire • *EK Success* kindergarten lettering template • Craft knife • Black fine tip pen • Glue dots

TIPS: Trim Kraft cardstock to 11" square and place on Green. Secure corners with a nailheads. Cut letters from Green cardstock, mount on Dark Green and trim. Hand write 'awesome' on White, trim and mount on Dark Green and Green. Mount photos on Dark Green and Green. Accent the sides of the photos with sequins and wire loops. Add frogs and wire squiggles as shown.

Wire Accents

Make spirals, curlicues and fireworks or wrap a simple shape with wire.

Add Shimmer with Wire!

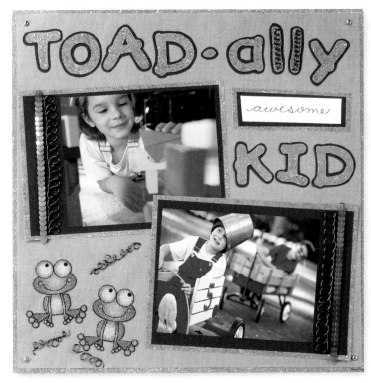

Create a Garden Bugs Border with Vellum & Wire!

Dragonfly Pattern

Fold

Butterfly Pattern

Fold

Bee Pattern

Fold

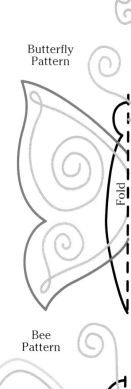

Tall Oaks *by Valoree Albert*
MATERIALS: Cardstock (Olive, Brown, Natural) • *Mary Engelbreit©* Green print paper and sticker • Vellum • *JewelCraft* (6 Gold 6mm spiral nailheads; 2 Green eyelets) • 24 gauge Bare Copper wire • 3 wood leaf buttons • Eyelet setter • Stick • Jute • Black fine tip pen • Pop dots
TIPS: Trim patterned paper to 11½" square and place on Brown. Crumple Olive and tear piece for journaling. Mount photo on Natural and crumpled cardstock. Mount sticker on White and Olive, trim and mount on Brown with pop dots. Set eyelets at top, thread twine and tie twig at top of page. Secure in several places with wire. Journal on vellum and mount on Natural and Brown. Place crumpled paper on left edge. Swirl wire by hand and secure over crumpled paper with nailheads. Add buttons.

If Friends... *by Valoree Albert*
MATERIALS: Cardstock (Brown, Tan) • Yellow dot print paper • Green sequin leaves • 24 gauge wire (Pink, Purple, Magenta) • Black fine tip pen • Gem-Tac • Pop dots
TIPS: Cut 1" strips of Tan, miter corners and glue on paper for frame. Glue Tan across bottom of paper. Make wire spirals for flowers. Arrange flower and leaves. Cut basket and attach with pop dots.

by Dona Tuscy

Butterfly - MATERIALS: Black cardstock • Aqua vellum • 28 gauge wire (Black, Green) • Pop dots

Dragonfly - MATERIALS: Black cardstock • Pink vellum • Wire (28 gauge Magenta, 24 gauge Black) • ½" circle punch • Pop dots

Bee - MATERIALS: Cardstock (Black, Yellow) • Yellow vellum • Wire (28 gauge Gold, 24 gauge Black) • ½" circle punch • Pop dots

Fancy Free *by Valoree Albert*

MATERIALS: Cardstock (White dot, Plum, Dark Purple) • *JewelCraft* (10mm Amethyst rhinestone; 12 Purple eyelets) • 26 gauge wire (Grape, Magenta, Light Brown) • Eyelet setter • Wire Worker tool with thin dowel • Round-nose pliers • Glue dots • Computer generated journaling

TIPS: Computer print title on White cardstock, trim and mount on Plum and Dark Purple. Mount photo on White and Dark Purple. Print journaling on White, trim and mount on Dark Purple. Make butterfly using wire tool and thin dowel. Shape coils to form wings. Glue rhinestone for head. Use small pieces of wire to attach butterfly. Use round-nose pliers to shape antenna. Hand swirl butterfly's path using Violet wire. Make coil border with Grape wire and eyelets.

Shape Coils

1. Carefully shape the coil while removing from the dowel.

2. Twist the ends of the wire to secure.

Secure Wire

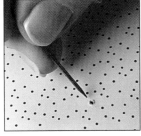 

1. Make a hole in the paper with a needle.

2. Insert the wire ends and twist on back.

Add Beads

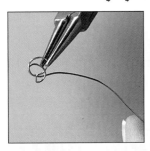 

1. Make a loop in ends of the wire using pliers.

2. Thread the beads on the wire.

Wedding... *by Valoree Albert*

MATERIALS: Cardstock (Silver, Plum) • Vellum • 24 gauge wire (Gold, Blue, Grape, Tinned Copper) • Blue mix beads • 12" of ⅜" Silver ribbon • 1½" heart template • Wire Worker with small dowel • Craft knife • Metallic Silver gel pen

TIPS: Mat photo on Plum. Cut heart in vellum so opening is over hands. Attach with beaded Silver wire. Make coils with remaining wires, stretch and tie together with ribbon. Glue bow on page.

Wire Accents

Vines twine, flowers bloom and bugs fly with the twist of a piece of wire!

Add Wire Spirals & Swirls!

Candle Pattern

Cupcake Pattern

Birthday Girl Star Jig Pattern

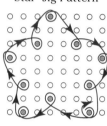

Birthday Girl   *by Erin Terrell*

MATERIALS: Cardstock (Dark Pink, Purple, Green, White, Yellow) • White velvet paper • *JewelCraft* (Bugle beads - Blue, Purple, Green; Yellow seed beads; 2 Amethyst 8mm rhinestones • 24 gauge Grape wire • *Scrap Pager* lettering templates (blockhead, whimsey, upper and lower case) • Wire jig • Wire Writer • Craft knife • Needle and thread • Orchid pen • Purple chalk • Foam mounting squares

TIPS: Make stars with jig and sew in place. Glue bugle beads on velvet paper for frosting and seed beads on flames. Cut out letters and outline with a pen.

Flag & Star Jig Pattern

Additional Patterns for a Jig

Kite Jig Diagram

Dogbone Jig Diagram

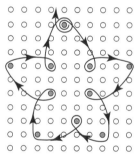

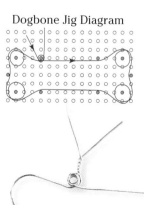

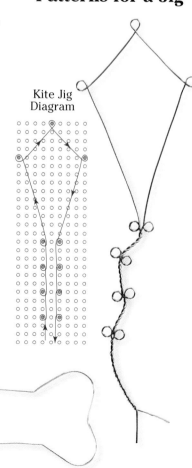

Flag & Stars   *by Deb Ringquist*

MATERIALS: Cardstock (Blue, White) • *Design Originals* print paper (Gold stars on Ivory, Stars & Stripes on Ivory) • *JewelCraft* FabricPuff White heart applique; Caviar Bead flag applique; 4 Silver 6mm nailheads; 4mm Ruby rhinestone; Seed beads - Red, White, Blue • Wire (Red, Tinned Copper, Blue) • Wire jig • Wire Writer • Black fine tip pen • Mini glue dots

TIPS: Cut border and attach with nailhead. Make wire stars and glue in place. Assemble page as shown.

Think Spring *by Valoree Albert*

MATERIALS: Cardstock (Green, Ivory) • *Provo Craft* paper • *Scrap Pagerz* party lettering template • 24 gauge wire (Rose, Kelly Green) • Wire Jig • Wire Writer • Round-nose pliers • Craft knife • Glue dots • Black fine tip pen

TIPS: Cut Ivory cardstock letters, mount on Green and trim. Tear strip of Ivory paper and place on left side. Make wire border using jig and Kelly Green wire. Place border on Ivory strip. Accent with spirals made from Rose wire. Make flowers with Rose. Hand shape leaf using Christmas Green. Mount flower on Ivory and accent center with sequins.

Think Spring Flower Jig Pattern

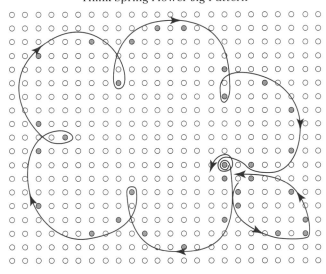

Daisy - age three
This was Daisy's first taste of watermelon for the season. She thought it was so yummy! She loves fruit so much, but watermelon is by far her favorite. She kept asking for it all Summer long.

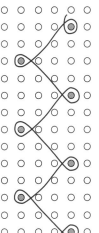

Wire on a Jig

With a wire jig, you can make borders, flowers, stars and frames with just a few twists and a minimum of time.

continued on pages 32-34

Think Spring Border Jig Pattern

Summer Photo Frame Jig Pattern

Summer *by Erin Terrell*

MATERIALS: Cardstock (Blue, Green, Black, Red, Light Blue) • Green plaid paper • *JewelCraft* (3 Red 9mm brads; Black seed beads) • 1½" letter template • 24 gauge Black wire • Wire jig • Wire Writer • Needle and thread • Sandpaper • Blue pen

TIP: Sand Blue paper to give it a rustic look. Make wire border and sew in place. Glue beads on title letters for seeds.

TIPS: Following diagram, place pegs in jig. Form a loop in wire end. Place loop on first peg. Wrap wire around pegs to form words or designs. Add beads to wire if desired. Use a needle and thread (or glue) to attach words to page.

Man Jig Diagram

Apple Jig Diagram

Lips Jig Diagram

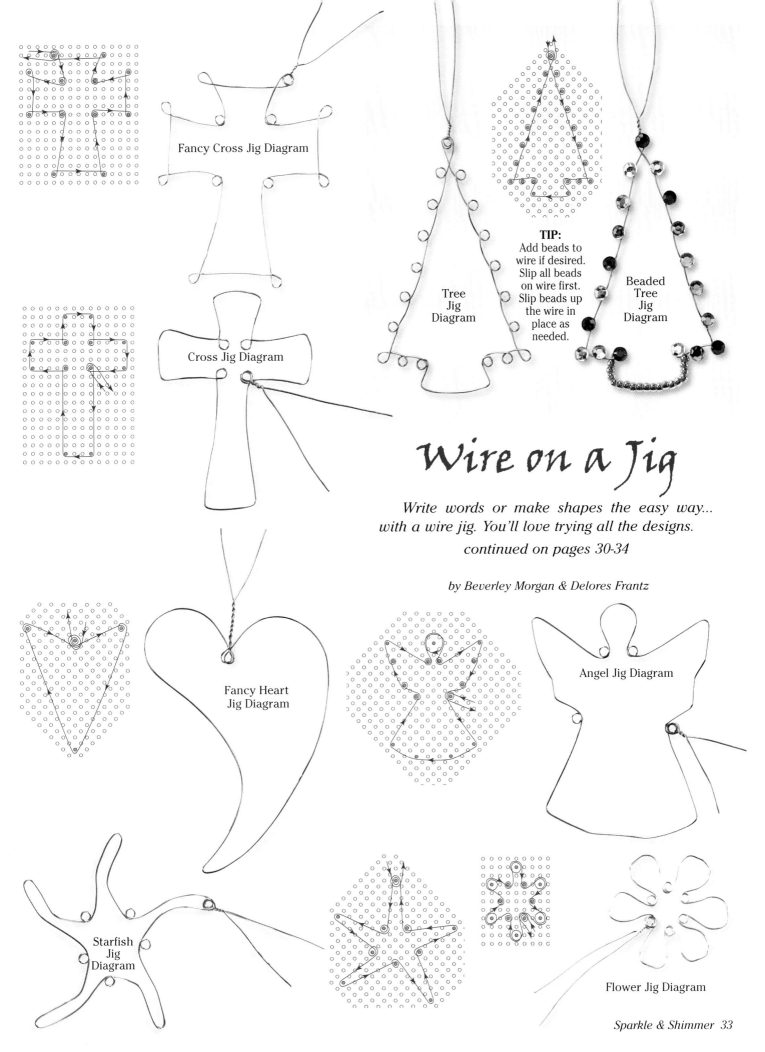

Fancy Cross Jig Diagram

Cross Jig Diagram

Tree Jig Diagram

TIP:
Add beads to wire if desired. Slip all beads on wire first. Slip beads up the wire in place as needed.

Beaded Tree Jig Diagram

Wire on a Jig

Write words or make shapes the easy way... with a wire jig. You'll love trying all the designs.

continued on pages 30-34

by Beverley Morgan & Delores Frantz

Fancy Heart Jig Diagram

Angel Jig Diagram

Starfish Jig Diagram

Flower Jig Diagram

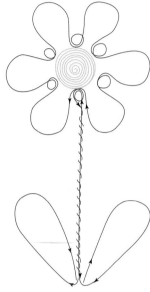

Wire on a Jig

Make any shape with a wire jig. Just draw a pattern, insert the pegs and wrap!

Using a Wire Jig

It's easy as 1-2-3! Just follow these easy steps to wonderful wire creations.

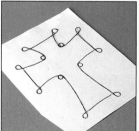

1. Copy, trace or draw a wire jig pattern.

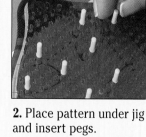

2. Place pattern under jig and insert pegs.

3. Thread the wire in the Wire Writer.

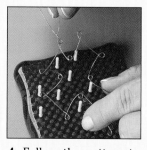

4. Follow the pattern to make the design.

Spring *by Delores Frantz*

MATERIALS: Green cardstock • *Design Originals* Green Scrappin' paper • Green grass die-cut • 20 gauge wire (Dark Green, Lemon, Tangerine, Rose, Aqua, Burgundy, Purple) • Wire jig • Wire Writer • Wire cutters • Round-nose pliers • Needle and thread • Stamp scissors
TIPS: Make flowers using jig. Form leaves and twist wires together to make stems. Make the spirals for the centers.

Additional Patterns for a Jig

continued on pages 30-33

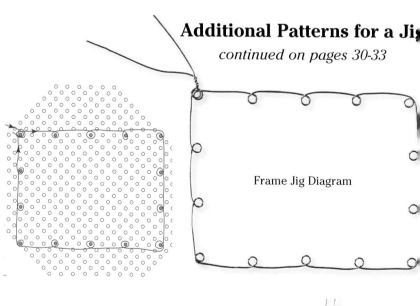

Frame Jig Diagram

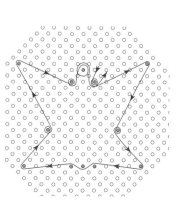

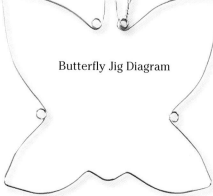

Butterfly Jig Diagram